Presents

People in the Play:

TIM   RUTH

SCENE: *A comfortable lounge room.*
TIM *bursts into the room where* RUTH *is reading. He carries a ragged old doll and an even more ragged zip-up bag.*

TIM: I'm back, Ruth!

RUTH: So?

TIM: Just thought you'd like to know.

RUTH: [*Goes back to reading her book.*] I don't.

TIM: [*excitedly.*] Look what I bought you at the rummage sale. [*Proudly holds up the doll.*]

RUTH: [*disgusted.*] Yuck! What's *that*?

TIM: What does it *look* like?

RUTH: I'm at a loss for words.

TIM: She only needs a little tidying up.
Anyway, with your birthday just around
the corner, I knew you'd like a new
doll... even if it's a bit old...

RUTH: ...and very dirty. How much did you
pay for it?

TIM: You shouldn't ask the cost of
presents, even when you don't like them.

RUTH: I know you were flat broke two
days ago, so it couldn't have been much.

TIM: Does it really matter what it cost?
The point is that I went to the rummage
sale, thought of you, and bought you a
doll. Believe me, there were plenty of
other things I could have spent my
hard-earned money on!

RUTH: You should have then. [*Picks up the
doll.*] I'll call her Grimy. [*Looks at her
and puts her down again.*]

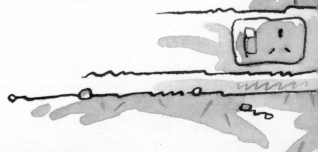

TIM: You won't recognize her after a good cleaning.

RUTH: Wouldn't want to. Anyway, thanks for buying me a present. If you weren't my little brother, I'd kiss you for being so sweet.

TIM: I'm glad I'm your brother.

RUTH: And what great present did you get for yourself?

TIM: [*Shows her the bag.*] This horrible zip-up bag.

RUTH: What on earth do you want such a thing for?

TIM: One never knows when a horrible zip-up bag may come in handy.

RUTH: [*Faces the audience and taps the side of her head.*] He's mad.

TIM: It's the only thing I could afford after I paid for your doll. [*Rattles the bag.*] Listen, there's something inside.

RUTH: Haven't you opened it yet?

TIM: Can't — it's jammed.

RUTH: [*Takes bag and looks at it.*] The zipper's rusted. [*Rattles the bag.*] Probably rubbish.

TIM: Or it could be diamonds and emeralds!

RUTH: Grow up, Tim. You don't find treasure at a rummage sale.

TIM: You never know. Some people do strange things...

RUTH: Some people *buy* strange things! [*Takes a small bottle of oil out of her pocket.*] I'm sure Mom won't mind. This should do the trick.

TIM: What trick?

RUTH: Watch, and you might learn something from an expert. [*She puts some oil on the zipper and slowly begins to open it.*]

TIM: [*Quickly takes bag away from her.*] It's *my* bag and *I'll* be the first to look inside! [*Opens it slowly and looks in.*]

RUTH: I bet it's not diamonds and emeralds.

TIM: No, but... [*Slight pause, then quickly.*] it's a rat covered in maggots! LOOK! [*Moves bag quickly to her face.*]

RUTH: [*Screams at the top of her voice.*] EEEEEEEEK! I loathe, hate, and detest rats! Mom! MOM! Tim's got a rat. Tim! Tim! You know I hate rats! Take it away you horrible boy!

TIM: [*Takes bag away.*] I was only putting you on, Ruth. Don't die of a heart attack!

RUTH: If I did, I'd blame *you*! So what's in the bag? I knew it wasn't a rat...

TIM: Well, look at this! It's a very old pair of glasses. [*Pulls them out and studies them.*] And they're just what I needed.

RUTH: What you need is a brain in working order! [TIM *puts on the glasses and* RUTH *begins to laugh loudly.*]

TIM: Go on, laugh. Laugh as much and as long as you like. It doesn't bother me in the least. I know I did well, and that's all that matters.

RUTH: [*Rocking with laughter.*] You paid *money* for *these*? [*Still laughing.*] You look like something out of a wax museum! [*Keeps laughing.*]

TIM: Wait a minute! [*Darts around the room carefully looking at things.*] This is AMAZING! I don't believe it! I just don't believe it!

RUTH: [*Suddenly stops laughing.*] What's amazing? What don't you believe?

TIM: [*Still looking around.*] What I see. [*pause.*] It can't be. WOW! [*Now stares at a blank wall very close up.*] This is absolutely incredible! What amazing luck!

RUTH: What are you going on about, Tim?

TIM: These glasses! They're *magic*! M. A. G. I. K.

RUTH: Apart from the fact that you can't spell, I don't believe you. [*pause.*] But tell me about it anyway.

TIM: I can see through things — solid things. I can see through chairs, through tables, through walls, through ceilings, through thick heads ...

RUTH: [*worried.*] Can you see through clothes?

TIM: [*Grins as he stares at her.*] If I want to.

RUTH: [*Quickly stands sideways.*] All right, let's run a test. [*Points to a spot on the wall.*] Look through *this*. What can you see?

TIM: [*focuses.*] Easy. The fridge.

RUTH: You knew it was there anyway!

TIM: [*refocuses.*] Maybe I did, but I can also see *inside* the fridge. There's a watermelon, a chicken lying comfortably on its side, some leftover potatoes just beginning to turn green, two tomatoes, six eggs, the custard tart you're saving, and a half eaten carton of strawberry yogurt with the lid left off.

RUTH: You always know what's inside the fridge! Give them to me! [*Snatches glasses from him, puts them on, and stares at him.*] I can't see through your clothes! [*Looks around the room.*] I can't see through anything!

TIM: What do you expect for five cents?

RUTH: Tim! You made the whole thing up! You're the world's biggest liar!

TIM: All right, next time there's a rummage sale at my school, you go. I'll stay home and poke holes in everything.

RUTH: I'd buy you a water pistol that squirts backwards! [*Picks the doll up roughly and starts to leave.*] Come on, Grimy, it's time for your bath, then I'll introduce you to Monica and Celia. [*Exit* RUTH.]

TIM: Lucky you. [*Puts glasses back on.*] It's quite amazing, what one can see. [*Looks around the room, then focuses on the audience.*] But I guess magic doesn't work for everyone.